TO RUN AND NOT GROW TIRED

Fran Sciacca

NAVPRESS

A MINISTRY OF THE NAVIGATORS
P.O. BOX 35001, COLORADO SPRINGS, COLORADO 80935

The Navigators is an international Christian organization. Jesus Christ gave His followers the Great Commission to go and make disciples (Matthew 28:19). The aim of The Navigators is to help fulfill that commission by multiplying laborers for Christ in every nation.

NavPress is the publishing ministry of The Navigators. NavPress publications are tools to help Christians grow. Although publications alone cannot make disciples or change lives, they can help believers learn biblical discipleship, and apply what they learn to their lives and ministries.

Unless otherwise identified, all Scripture in this publication is from the *Holy Bible: New International Version* (NIV). Copyright © 1973, 1978, 1984, International Bible Society. Used by permission of Zondervan Bible Publishers. Other versions used include: the *Good News Bible: Today's English Version* (TEV), copyright © American Bible Society 1966, 1971, 1976; the *New American Standard Bible* (NASB), © The Lockman Foundation 1960, 1962, 1963, 1968, 1971, 1972, 1973, 1975, 1977; and the *King James Version* (KJV).

Printed in the United States of America

10 11 12 13 14 15 16 17/99 98 97 96

CONTENTS

INTRODUCTION

Therefore, since we are surrounded by such a great cloud of witnesses, let us throw off everything that hinders and the sin that so easily entangles, and let us run with perseverance the race marked out for us. Let us fix our eyes on Jesus, the author and perfecter of our faith . . . so that you will not grow weary and lose heart.

Hebrews 12:1-3

The spiritual journey of life is in many ways like a marathon we are running. The race itself is often exhilarating, full of the kind of passion and adventure that we would never experience from the passive vantage point of an armchair on the sidelines. Yet as we make our way through the long and winding course, we often sustain certain spiritual injuries that we could never have anticipated, and don't know how to cure.

As the great physician of the soul, God has "inside knowledge" about how to bring healing to the unique set of difficult circumstances we find ourselves in. His Word contains relevant, therapeutic truth for our trauma, hurt, and depression. Sometimes it seems that the circle of pain can have an ever expanding influence, spreading its ominous shadow over every aspect of

5

our lives. But God is able to help us, especially when we're limping or crawling instead of running through the race.

A number of years ago I wrote *To Walk and Not Grow Weary*, focusing on problems experienced by biblical characters—problems we still encounter today. *To Run and Not Grow Tired* continues the process of looking at how God understands our personal problems and guides us into His balanced, timely solutions.

To Run and Not Grow Tired is designed to help restore your soul by redirecting your focus—back to Jesus, "the author and perfecter of our faith." It contains twelve cameos of God's people under pressure—men and women of faith who survived life's adversity and stand before us now as testimonies of the eternal grace of God. They are the "cloud of witnesses" whose lives can be a source of insight, strength, and promise as we look to God to give us His strength when we feel too tired and overwhelmed to go on in the race He has called us to run.

1. HANNAH

Coping With Criticism

ABIDING PRINCIPLE

The best way to deal with the verbal abuse and harsh criticism of others is to talk about it with God.

Patience is the ability to put up with people you'd like to put down. —Ulrike Ruffert

LOOKING AT HANNAH

It is sometimes difficult to say which hurts more: physical or verbal abuse. At least when someone hits you, your body responds by bleeding, swelling, or bruising. There is some evidence so that others can see that you've truly been hurt. But words leave no such obvious indication of injury. In fact, the real damage done by harsh words often shows up long after they were actually said.

This painful process is accentuated when the verbal assaults are regular and continual. It is discouraging indeed to have to face someone day after day who makes it a religious duty to be verbally harsh, critical, and exasperating.

Such was the case with Hannah, the barren wife of a man named Elkanah. Unfortunately for Hannah, Elkanah had another wife, Peninnah, who happened to be as fertile as the Jordan Valley! It would have been bad enough for Hannah to have to share her husband in a home where the sound of children's voices was a steady reminder of her childlessness. But poor Hannah also had to put up with constant harassment from "her rival." Peninnah "provoked her till she wept and would not eat." Instead of her home being a place of dignity and solace, Hannah's was one of torment and humiliation.

Yet, her godly way of handling that constant verbal onslaught stands as a sterling reminder that knowing God can make all the difference in the world in the face of life's criticism and humiliation.

SCRIPTURE 1 Samuel 1:1–2:11
_____

STUDY QUESTIONS
_____

1. How serious would you say Hannah's hurt was? Support your response from the passage.

2. What evidence can you find in this story to indicate that Peninnah's actions and words were intentional and malicious?

3. In what ways do you think her husband actually added to Hannah's pain rather than alleviating it (1 Samuel 1:4-8)?

4. When we are wounded by the words of others, our greatest temptation is to talk about our hurt or malign the reputation of the one inflicting it. What does Hannah do? Why is this so significant?

5. How can you best explain 1 Samuel 1:18, considering that nothing tangible has changed and Hannah will be returning to the same home with the same people and problems?

6. Look at Hannah's prayer in 1 Samuel 2:1-10. Omitting her references to childbirth, find several statements that refer to God's character and ultimate justice. List them in the chart.

Statements About God's Character	Verses

Statements About Ultimate Justice	Verses

LEARNING FROM HANNAH

Any person whose condition is described with the words "bitterness of soul," "misery," and "great anguish and grief" is not experiencing just a bad day on the job! Hannah was wounded and crushed by the continual harassment of people in her own home. Her husband added insult to injury by not restraining the woman who attacked her daily. Elkanah offered Hannah gifts and sought to take her mind off her pain rather than talking to her openly and sensitively about it.

The only solace Hannah found was in the presence of the Lord, pouring out her complaint to Him in the temple. And even there she was falsely accused by Eli the priest of being drunk!

While it is true that Hannah desperately wanted a son and begged God for one, it is also true that when she left to return to Ramah, she had no assurance of an answer from God, only the blessing of Eli, which was little more than a perfunctory benediction.

Hannah's comfort and encouragement came from "pouring out [her] soul to the LORD . . . out of [her] great anguish and grief." It was by spending time in God's presence that she regained the strength to face Peninnah. And in so doing, Hannah set the course for those of us who find ourselves in similar circumstances of inner pain.

APPLICATION QUESTIONS

7. In general, would you characterize the way you talk to others as sarcasm and criticism, or as healing and encouragement? Explain.

8. a. Who is the "Peninnah" in your life right now? (Perhaps *you* are the person most critical of yourself.) How does your response to this person compare with Hannah's?

   b. What needs to change? To continue?

9. Perhaps you are a "Peninnah" for someone else. If so, write out, as best you can, how you should treat the "Hannah" in your life. Describe what needs to change and how you intend to go about it.

• The needed changes:

• The proposed plan:

SCRIPTURE MEMORY

Dealing with criticism — 1 Peter 2:23
Speaking constructively — Ephesians 4:29

2. PETER

Failing Someone You Love

ABIDING PRINCIPLE

Putting too much confidence in others or in yourself will always lead to dashed expectations and fractured relationships.

In prosperity our friends know us; in adversity we know our friends. —Churton Collins

LOOKING AT PETER

The apostle Peter was a man of intense passion. He invested 100 percent of himself in everything he did. People like Peter, who live on the rim of extremes, are always familiar with both the exhilaration of success and the sting of defeat because of the sense of abandon with which they approach all of life.

Peter experienced miraculous "jail-breaks," Pentecostal fire, evangelistic revival, and intense persecution. He was one of the "inner three" disciples, and an eyewitness of both the transfigured and the resurrected Jesus Christ.

Peter was fiercely devoted to Jesus. He was also

the most outspoken about his commitment! Peter announced that he would die for his Master if need be—a promise he was no doubt willing to fulfill.

In spite of the depth of his commitment and the fervor of his devotion, Peter failed our Lord in a profoundly personal way. It was not neglect of duty—failure to do what you're told. Peter's failure was a breach of trust—the conscious denial of the bond of love. At a time when Jesus needed Peter, he denied three times that he even knew Him!

Consequently, Peter remains forever as an example of what to expect from others and ourselves when we place security in people rather than in God.

SCRIPTURE Matthew 26:57-75

STUDY QUESTIONS

1. Examine the following passages. Think carefully as you read them a couple of times. Then, write what you learn about Peter. Pay special attention for insights about Peter's estimate of himself.

   Mark 8:31-34

   John 13:1-9

Mark 14:27-31

2. Mark 14:32-42 further describes the circumstances surrounding Peter's denial of Jesus. Read this passage carefully and record what helps to further explain Peter's failure.

3. a. Peter violently confronted the temple guard in the garden of Gethsemane as they prepared to arrest Jesus (John 18:1-11). He undoubtedly believed that this was his opportunity to die for Jesus, and he was ready! Yet just a few hours later, Peter publicly denied that he even knew Jesus. Look at Mark 14:66-72. Who actually "unraveled" Peter and initiated the process that ended in his disgrace?

b. What principle can you draw from this situation about the temptation to fail those we love? (Keep in mind how "prepared" Peter was in the garden.)

4. How do you think Peter felt when the rooster crowed (Mark 14:72)? Why?

5. John 21:15-19 contains a beautiful ending to this story. Describe this glorious message of hope for times when we "fail" in our relationship with God.

6. There is genuine encouragement in knowing that God will always forgive us when we fail Him. But

what about when we fail others or they fail us? Is there always a guarantee of restoration? Are there any safeguards to prevent it from happening? Look up the verses below and write out at least one principle from each that can apply to this issue of failing others and others failing us.

Verses	Principle
Proverbs 18:19	
Proverbs 20:6	
Isaiah 2:22	
John 2:23-25	
Romans 15:1	
Colossians 3:13	

LEARNING FROM PETER

Peter possessed an inflated view of his understanding and commitment that was compounded by a weak grasp of his own frailty and sin. He actually believed that there were some sins he was incapable of committing! Consequently, he was prepared for the obvious but vulnerable to the unexpected. His boasting gave way to cowardice in the blinking of an eye, and he denied the Lord he had promised to die for.

But God knows that failure and sin are part and parcel of our fallen nature. So He restores us whenever we repent and ask for forgiveness. Three times Jesus gave Peter the chance to affirm his love for Him—the same number of times he had denied Him. The twofold message for us today is that people constantly fail God and each other. What we do with this message of failure is up to us.

APPLICATION QUESTIONS

7. Have you failed God in a significant way lately? How? Are you willing to let Him "restore" you?

8. Are there any sins that you honestly believe you could or would never commit? If so, list some of the main ones below. Explain why you feel this way.

9. Describe how someone has failed you recently.

10. How do you think God wants you to handle this situation?

11. Here is a partial list of ways we tend to fail others. Check all the ones that describe a recent failure on your part. In the space provided, put the initials of the person you failed.

❑ Not keeping secrets. _____

❑ Breaking promises. _____

❑ Not defending someone I love. _____

❑ Not forgiving. _____

❑ Talking behind someone's back. _____

❑ Not being honest. _____

❑ Unrealistic expectations. _____

❑ Criticizing. _____

❑ Other: _____

12. Look over the above list. Pick someone you've failed in one of these ways. Then write out what needs to change so that you don't continue failing that person, and how you intend to go about it.

SCRIPTURE MEMORY

Trusting in people—Isaiah 2:22
Being responsible to those you've failed—Matthew 5:23-24

3. SARAH

Misplaced Hope

ABIDING PRINCIPLE

Hope that is grounded in anything other than the unchanging character of God will cause you to become disillusioned and discouraged.

When you say a situation or a person is hopeless, you are slamming the door in the face of God. —Charles L. Allen

LOOKING AT SARAH

Literature abounds with stories of hope: heroes and heroines who braved life's storms, beat the odds, and saved the day. We all have our favorites. But usually these accounts are merely isolated shrines to a select few who somehow, for a few brief moments, possessed unusual cunning, fortitude, or stamina.

However, for most people, life contains a long line of dashed dreams and shattered hopes. Life is difficult, and for some people it seems to get more and more difficult all the time. How do we maintain a genuine sense of hope in the face of constant difficulty and disappointment?

Sarah, the wife of the patriarch Abraham, was challenged to hope against overwhelming odds. God promised her husband that he would be the father of many nations. But Sarah was old and barren! The study of her life reveals a pattern of behavior that is typical and familiar to us. Sarah finally rested her hope in the only proper place, but not until she had exhausted nearly every other possibility first.

SCRIPTURE Genesis 17:1-22, 18:1-15

STUDY QUESTIONS

1. Describe the importance of hope in our lives (Proverbs 13:12).

2. In your own words, summarize how Sarah probably felt when she found out what God had told her husband at the following four significant points in their lives.

Genesis 12:1-9 (age 65).

Genesis 15:1-5 (age 70).

Genesis 16:1-4,15-16 (age 76).

Genesis 17:1-8,15-22; 18:1-15 (age 90).

3. What progression can you see in Sarah's thinking? How does she try to preserve her hope?

4. Look up the following verses. Read each one carefully, and write down any insights you may glean on the nature of *hope*.

Verses	Insights About Hope
Psalm 31:24	
Psalm 39:7	
Romans 8:24	

Verses	Insights About Hope
Romans 15:4	
Hebrews 6:19	

5. Jeremiah contrasts two people who have their hope properly and improperly placed. In your own words, describe each.

   • Misplaced hope, or "trust" (Jeremiah 17:5-6):

   • Properly placed hope, or "trust" (Jeremiah 17:7-8):

LEARNING FROM SARAH

Sarah first sought to place her hope in anything but the unchanging character of God. She trusted in her own ability to conceive and bear children. But that eventually failed. Then she concocted a scheme that allowed her to dictate how and when God's promised son to Abraham would be born. But that, too, turned sour. Finally, Sarah "gave up" and concluded that God was either impotent or deceitful.

It was precisely at that point in her disillusionment that God appeared to Abraham with a message for his wife: Sarah would give birth to the son she could not bear on her own!

As she exhausted her own resources and plans, Sarah came face-to-face with the sobering truth that it is easy to hope in God when there is a chance that we can fulfill His promises. But such hope is not rooted in God's unchanging character. It is merely an extension of our own abilities, combined with some vague notions about God.

APPLICATION QUESTIONS

6. Describe a time when you felt or acted like Sarah recently.

7. Do you think it is possible to maintain genuine hope in God when things go from bad to worse instead of improving? Explain.

8. Look back at Paul's statement about cultivating and nurturing hope in Romans 15:4. Which of the two ingredients he mentions do you need to cultivate?

❑ Endurance.
❑ Encouragement from the Scriptures.

Write out what you need to do and how you plan to go about it.

9. Based on what you've learned from this lesson, what would you do differently if you were to meet another circumstance similar to the one you described in question 6?

10. Why is it that hope based on God's character becomes a foundation for all other types of hope (hope for the future, hope for success, etc.)?

SCRIPTURE MEMORY

The ingredients for cultivating hope—Romans 15:4
The focus of your hope—Psalm 39:7

4. CAIN

Self-Pity: A Doorway to Destruction

ABIDING PRINCIPLE

Feeling sorry for yourself is the first step on a downward staircase of destructive emotions and behavior.

When a man is all wrapped up in himself he makes a pretty small package. —John Ruskin

LOOKING AT CAIN

Cain and Abel were the first children born of human parents. Little did the proud parents, Adam and Eve, realize that the names of these two boys would become synonymous with everything that can go wrong in a family. Cain and Abel experienced sibling rivalry at its worst. They stand as a classic example of human conflict.

But although we're all familiar with what happened, few of us understand the cause of Cain's anger. What was it that drove him to kill his own brother that terrible day in the field? Even though it's not clearly stated in the biblical account, enough clues are present for us to come up with a possible explanation. And even more importantly, the tragic life of Cain provides us with a warning about similar tendencies in our own lives.

SCRIPTURE Genesis 4:1-17
_____

STUDY QUESTIONS
_____

1. a. Explain briefly which of the two young men had the hardest life, and why. Be creative. (See Genesis 4:2, and also Genesis 1:29-30 and 3:17-19. *Hint:* People didn't begin to eat meat until after the Flood. See Genesis 9:1-3.)

   b. In what way could this have prompted Cain to feel sorry for himself?

2. Self-pity always begins with someone making comparisons with someone else. How do you see this to be true in the case of Cain (Genesis 4:3-5)?

3. God meets Cain at an emotional crossroads in Genesis 4:6-7. What are Cain's options at this point? What is God's counsel?

   • Cain's options:

   • God's counsel:

4. Self-pity's typical pattern is presented below. Trace this pattern in the life of Cain using the following four steps.

   Step 1—I compare myself to someone else, and conclude that life is not "fair."

   Step 2—I resist the truth about myself.

   Step 3—I cast blame rather than admit guilt.

Step 4—I become angry at others (including God), and isolate myself.

5. In Luke 15:11-32, we see a profound parable told by Jesus. The younger son (the "prodigal son") had his own problems with rebellion. But we see something about the nature of self-pity in the attitude and behavior of the older son (verses 28-30). Read this passage and describe the similarities you see in the rivalry between these brothers and the rivalry between Cain and Abel.

6. In 2 Corinthians 10:3-7, Paul gives some sound counsel regarding spiritual warfare. One of his comments contains a principle that can be applied to our battle with self-pity: "We demolish arguments and every pretension that sets itself up against the knowledge of God, and we take captive every thought to make it obedient to Christ." Write out what you can see in this passage that tells where the battle for self-pity must be fought, and some insights about how to fight it.

7. What basic truth about comparing and complaining do you see in Romans 9:20-21?

LEARNING FROM CAIN

Cain concluded that life was somehow unfair. His brother "had it all," or so it seemed to him. While Cain sweated and toiled trying to keep back the weeds and thistles from his crops (the byproduct of his parents' disobedience!), his younger brother sat in the shade tending the flocks. Cain's family depended on him for food, but Abel's sheep and goats were mere "luxuries"! (Remember, man didn't eat meat until after the Flood.)

Cain truly lost the ability to think clearly and his world shrunk to a circumference large enough for only one: himself! Self-pity is an addictive mind-set that often leads to regrettable conduct—in this case, the death of an only brother.

None of us are immune from the threatening tentacles of self-pity. The tendency to compare our lot in life with that of those around us is still a tempting option dangling before us daily. Whether it be a better job, a healthier body, a more understanding spouse, a larger home, or a fatter bank account, we are tempted to compare what God has given us to what He has given someone else. We, too, can lose the ability to think clearly. And we, too, can behave as destructively as Cain—if not toward others, at least toward ourselves.

8. Describe a recent bout with self-pity from your own life. Use the four-step pattern of behavior from question 4 in the first section.

9. Who do you tend to neglect most when you are feeling sorry for yourself? Why?

10. Do you have a harder time when you compare yourself to other Christians or to nonbelievers? Explain.

11. Some of the best "antidotes" for self-pity are:

❑ confessing it as sin.
❑ being honest with God regularly about your feelings.
❑ reading and memorizing Scripture.
❑ getting involved in the needs of others.
❑ talking it over with a close, objective friend.

If you have been battling self-pity lately, pick at least two of these courses of action, and then write out what you intend to do and when.

12. Perhaps you don't struggle with self-pity but know of someone who does. How can you help that person find the way out of the mire of feeling sorry for himself or herself? (You may want to consider one or more of the above "antidotes.")

SCRIPTURE MEMORY

The seriousness of self-pity—Genesis 4:7
A solution for self-pity—Philippians 2:4

5. JEZEBEL

The Appetite for Control Over Others

ABIDING PRINCIPLE

If you insist on controlling those under your authority rather than serving them, you will sacrifice the joy of leadership on the altar of power.

To command is to serve, nothing more and nothing less.
—André Malraux

LOOKING AT JEZEBEL

Nearly nine centuries before Christ, Ahab, king of Israel, married the daughter of the pagan king of a neighboring country. During the twenty-two years of his reign, the name of his wife became a household word—or more accurately, a household curse!—*Jezebel*.

Jezebel manipulated everyone she came into contact with, and repeatedly defied the Word of God spoken through the prophet Elijah. Jezebel always got her way, and woe unto those unfortunate enough to get in her way! Her happiness depended on being on top of others. She abides forever within the record of

Scripture as an embodiment of a power-hungry and unteachable heart.

SCRIPTURE 1 Kings 21:4-16

STUDY QUESTIONS

1. Below is a partial list of the people and spheres that were under Jezebel's control (either obvious or covert). Ponder each passage carefully, and record your observations on how she exercised control. Use short phrases to describe her methods.

   • The prophets of God (1 Kings 18:3-4).

   • The false prophets of Baal and Asherah (1 Kings 18:19).

   • The elders at Jezreel (1 Kings 21:5-14).

   • Her husband, the king (1 Kings 21:7,15-16,25).

   • Elijah, the prophet of God (1 Kings 18:40, 19:1-4).

2. There was a character in the early church named Diotrephes who loved "to be first," to control other people (3 John 9-10). List some of the ways this man tried to manipulate people around him.

3. What can you deduce from the following passages about our "natural" tendencies regarding being in authority and power: Ephesians 5:22-2 Ephesians 6:1-9, Philippians 2:3-4, Colossians 3:19-21, Colossians 4:1, 1 Peter 5:2-3?

4. Why do you think we often take inappropriately aggressive, domineering approaches to power?

5. Jesus clearly states God's model of exercising authority and power in Luke 22:24-27. How does it differ from Jezebel's? (Think hard. Be thorough.)

LEARNING FROM JEZEBEL

Jezebel could easily have authored the book *The Art of Intimidation*. She enjoyed slamming her hand on the chessboard of life and watching the pieces jump and scatter at her beck and call. It shouldn't surprise us to discover that she was also deeply involved in witchcraft—the ultimate quest for control over others (2 Kings 9:22).

Jezebel's life stands as an extreme warning to us about the temptations facing people in positions of authority of any kind. And although few of us will ever experience the position of authority Jezebel held, each of us nevertheless has a sinful tendency to misuse and abuse power over others.

Jesus has made it abundantly clear through His teaching and His actions that godly authority serves rather than subjugates, gives rather than grabs, is selfless rather than selfish.

APPLICATION QUESTIONS

6. How do we maintain proper balance between our position of authority and power, and the practice of the duties associated with that position?

7. Below, check the boxes that describe a role in your life right now that has the potential to become a position in which you abuse authority, power, or control.

   ❑ Parent.   ❑ Spouse.   ❑ Manager.
   ❑ Teacher.   ❑ Employer.   ❑ Group leader.
   ❑ Supervisor.   ❑ Friend.   ❑ Elder in church.
   ❑ Fiancée.   ❑ Other: _____

8. Select three of the boxes you checked and indicate below whose style—Jesus' or Jezebel's—best characterizes your current behavior in that role.

Relationship 1 _____

My style: ❑ Jesus   ❑ Jezebel

Relationship 2 _____

My style: ❑ Jesus   ❑ Jezebel

Relationship 3 _____

My style: ❑ Jesus   ❑ Jezebel

9. Pick one of these three relationships and write out below how you can change your behavior if it resembles Jezebel's style, or how you can strengthen it if it resembles Jesus' style. Be specific.

• What I can do:

• How I can do it:

10. Perhaps you need to do more than merely change your own behavior. Maybe there's someone you've hurt through your desire to be in control. Talk to that person this week and explain what you've come to learn about yourself and godly leadership. Ask for forgiveness, if necessary.

Perhaps there's someone in a position of power in your life right now who is wounding others by his or her leadership style. Pray for that person each day this week, asking God to show him or her the value of servant leadership. Talk to that person, if necessary.

If there is someone in your life whose leadership style is an encouragement to you and others, tell that person so via a short note or phone call.

SCRIPTURE MEMORY

A principle of godly leadership—2 Corinthians 4:5
The practice of godly leadership—Luke 22:26-27

6. PAUL

Dealing With Your Past

The past is something to learn from and leave behind, not to dwell on and allow to dictate how you live today.

In the carriages of the past you can't go anywhere.
—Maxim Gorky

LOOKING AT PAUL

Memory is a marvelous faculty of the mind. It provides us with a perpetual feast of all that is cherished from our past. But it can also be a cruel taskmaster, emotionally blackmailing us with recollections we long to forget, but can't.

Much has been said recently about dealing with and relating to our painful past: healing memories, primal therapy, and codependence, to mention only a few. Does the Bible provide any insight for us as we try to deal with our complex web of tangled emotions?

Saul of Tarsus, known affectionately to us as the apostle Paul, provides us with a case study full of pain, yet radiant with hope and practical help. His own past was one of extremes. He experienced unusual successes and intense opposition and trials. He lived with a whole range of memories, both pleasant and painful. Yet his response was as down-to-earth and relevant as the morning news. Paul knew that his past was a powerful force in his life, but he also knew how to deal with it.

SCRIPTURE Philippians 3

STUDY QUESTIONS

1. Look at Paul's own description of his past religious affiliation in Philippians 3:5-6 and Acts 26:4-5. What can you deduce about him as a person from these passages?

2. Using your answer from question 1, what other possible insights about Saul the Pharisee may be drawn from Matthew 15:1-9, 21:45-46, 26:3-5, and 27:41-43?

3. Describe in as much detail as possible what Saul did (or might have done), based on the following accounts of his behavior.

Acts 7:54-60

Acts 8:1-3

Acts 9:1-2

4. Do you think Paul would have been better off if he had dealt with his past with a great deal of careful attention and therapy? Explain.

5. Look at 1 Corinthians 15:7-10 carefully and answer the following questions.

   • What evidence is there that Paul had not forgotten his past?

• How had Paul's past affected his perspective on the present?

6. a. The "secret" to Paul's dealing with his past is spelled out for us in Philippians 3:10-14. What is it?

   b. When you consider your answer to the first part of question 5, how do you explain Paul's phrase "forgetting what is behind"?

7. In light of what you've learned from the previous verses, what do you think Paul means in Philippians 3:15?

LEARNING FROM PAUL

Before his encounter with Jesus Christ, Paul's personal history was decorated with the emblems of worldly and "religious" success. But he also carried with him the stigma of being an enemy of God. He was personally responsible for fragmenting many Christian families, destroying churches, and perhaps even killing some of God's first-century faithful. These vivid recollections were the mental freight Paul carried with him always. So much did it occupy his thinking that he considered himself the "least of the apostles" as a result (1 Corinthians 15:9).

Yet Paul was not stuck in the mire of his past, be it good or bad! He said that he "forgot" what was behind and strained for the goal of being like Jesus, the very thing for which God had laid hold of him in the first place (Philippians 3:12-14).

Paul didn't forget his past. How could he? But he didn't massage, nourish, contemplate, and examine it. Instead, he used his past as a testimony to others and a continual reminder to himself that "by the grace of God I am what I am" (1 Corinthians 15:10).

APPLICATION QUESTIONS

8. Paul said he wanted to "know Christ and the power of his resurrection" (Philippians 3:10). What do you think that means, and how does one go about it?

9. Paul's focus was on the powerful *person of Christ* and the growth *process*, not a place or a time. In regard to painful memories, to what do you give most of your mental energy? Explain.

❏ A person in the past.
❏ A place in the past.
❏ A time in the past.
❏ The person of Jesus.
❏ The power of the resurrected Christ in your life.

10. Do you think that these principles apply to painful things that have happened since you've become a Christian as well? Explain.

11. a. What can you do, practically speaking, to "starve" the memory that is holding you back from "knowing Christ and the power of his resurrection"? (Read these passages on *God's Word* [Colossians 3:16, 2 Timothy 3:16-17, James 1:21-22], *prayer* [Psalm 62:8, Ephesians 6:18, Philippians 1:4-6,9-11], and *fellowship* [Acts 2:42-47, 1 John 1:3,6-7].)

b. What can you do to help a friend starve the memory that is holding him or her back from "knowing Christ and the power of his resurrection"?

12. How can you transform your perspective on your past to be a testimony to the grace of God?

SCRIPTURE MEMORY

Leaving the past behind—Isaiah 43:18-19
Knowing that God is your focus—Philippians 3:13-14

7. MARTHA

The Threat of Resentment

ABIDING PRINCIPLE

Resentment can be a clear indicator of misspent energy, misplaced service, or misguided enthusiasm, where we are more concerned about what other people think than about what God thinks.

Nothing on earth consumes a person more quickly than the passion of resentment. —Friedrich Nietzsche

LOOKING AT MARTHA

In Bethany, an obscure little village two miles from Jerusalem, two sisters and their brother shared a home. Martha, the eldest, was more or less the "head" of the household. Her younger sister, Mary, was thoughtful and meditative. Her main role was to provide help and assistance. The brother, Lazarus, was the recipient of their combined and constant care.

But one spring day, Jesus of Nazareth came to town, along with His disciples and a group of the devoted and curious. Bethany became His temporary home as He entered the final week of His earthly life.

On this particular visit of Jesus to her home, Martha decided to go "all out" for the Master. She planned a feast of great proportions. But in the midst of it all, she became angry and resentful of her younger sister, who seemed more interested in sitting than serving!

Martha stands forever as an illustration of the outcome of misplaced zeal and unrealistic expectations. And in so doing, she also provides us with vital insight into the nature and causes of a passion common to us all: *resentment.*

SCRIPTURE Luke 10:38-42; John 11:17-21, 12:1-3

STUDY QUESTIONS

---

1. How do you think Martha went about determining what "needed to be done" in regard to her dinner party?

2. a. The Greek word translated "distracted" (Luke 10:40) carries with it the idea of being pulled or dragged away, and being overburdened. What was overburdening and dragging Martha away?

b. Who was actually responsible for all the "work" Martha was "left to do" all by herself? What is one principle about a cause of resentment that can be gleaned from this story?

3. The temptation to become resentful seems especially relevant to those in any care-giving capacity. Paul told Timothy that those in the ministry must be careful not to become resentful (2 Timothy 2:24). Why might resentment be a temptation for those who are serving and helping others?

4. Paul's comments in Colossians 3:23-24 shed light on our tendency toward resentment. How can this perspective be applied to the problem of resentment, and why are the commands in this passage so important?

5. In the chart that follows are some additional verses that deal with resentment. Look up each one, and in your own words, write out *what* it is that we tend to resent and *why*.

What I Tend to Resent	Why
Proverbs 3:11-12	
Proverbs 19:3	

LEARNING FROM MARTHA

Martha plunged ahead to fulfill her own plan for meeting the "needs" of this group—as she perceived them. The unfortunate truth is that Martha had already decided for herself what the others needed, and then became resentful when no one helped her fulfill her vision. When we hear what Jesus said to her, we don't have to wonder too much what He would have told her had she simply asked Him what He needed or wanted when He first arrived.

Resentment hunts and haunts those who give to others. If we are not convinced that what we are sacrificing is what God wants, we will eventually be hurt and become resentful. Our motivation in sacrifice and service must be the Lord's commendation, never that of those to whom the service is rendered. Moreover, we must be careful to make sure that the "needs" we have determined worthwhile are truly needs to those we believe have them!

We must also be open to the Lord's correction and rebuke, whether it comes in the form of a comment from a friend, a message from the pulpit, or a passage from the Scriptures. Martha probably responded to the Lord's suggestion to shorten her "menu," and was not offended in the process. And by doing so, she cut off her resentment before it had opportunity to take root.

6. The first two words of Job 5:2 are, "Resentment kills." Why is resentment such a damaging emotion?

7. Below is a partial list of areas where resentment is common. Put a check beside the ones you struggle with.

❑ I am criticized more than commended.
❑ I have to do all the work to maintain a relationship.
❑ I am taken for granted by my children (or parents).
❑ I am taken for granted by my spouse (or girlfriend/boyfriend).
❑ I am taken for granted by my coworkers.
❑ I receive no help at my work place.
❑ I receive no help around the house.
❑ No one takes an interest in my life, but everyone expects me to be interested in theirs.
❑ I have no time to myself.
❑ Other _____

8. Look back at the items you've checked above. How many of them are due to:

• your own expectations or standards?
• improper motivation?
• not communicating with the other person(s)?

Select one or two, then write out what you need to do about this resentment and how you plan to go about it.

53

9. Perhaps you're in a position of authority or leadership in which others constantly serve you. Maybe you're a mother who heaps more responsibility on one child than on another. Look at the list in question 7, and circle two or three areas where you could minimize others' feelings of resentment by means of affirmation or action. Then write out what you intend to do, and how you plan to go about it.

10. How does this principle apply to relationships where there is a pattern of one person giving and one person taking?

11. How can you apply the principles from this lesson to help a friend who is resentful?

SCRIPTURE MEMORY

Guarding our emotions—Proverbs 4:23
Proper motivation for service—Colossians 3:23-24

8. KING SAUL

The Desire for Notoriety

ABIDING PRINCIPLE

The desire for recognition, popularity, and notoriety among people will eventually put you at odds with God Himself.

God sends no one away empty except those who are full of themselves. —Dwight L. Moody

LOOKING AT SAUL

In many of our relationships we are not afforded the benefit of the "long view" —the opportunity to see the beginning and end of people's lives, as well as everything in between. Consequently, we often arrive at premature conclusions about people that in the final analysis are totally mistaken. This is as true of our ideas about new believers as it is about presidential candidates.

Following the period of the Judges, God's people wanted to be like the neighboring countries. They clamored for a king (1 Samuel 8:1-5). They wanted someone "larger than life," with an impressive appearance and a charismatic personality. God reluctantly granted their persistent request, setting His approval on the tall, strong, handsome young man that the people found so appealing. And so Saul became Israel's first king. God gave him His Spirit, and He "changed" him (1 Samuel 10:6).

But soon Saul got carried away with his official power, and gradually changed in a different way. He was driven by the desire to be in charge, to be noticed, to be "somebody." The real outcome of such an outlook is preserved forever in the words of Saul himself near the end of his life: "Surely I have acted like a fool and have erred greatly" (1 Samuel 26:21).

SCRIPTURE 1 Samuel 9:1-2, 13:1-14, 15:1-34

STUDY QUESTIONS

1. Saul had natural abilities that were further augmented by divine gifts from God. Using the "Scripture" passages from 1 Samuel listed above, combine your insights to construct a paragraph on "A Profile of King Saul."

Saul's Natural Abilities
9:2
9:20-21

56

Saul's Supernatural Endowments

10:6

10:7

10:26

11:6

A Profile of King Saul

2. Saul was chosen and appointed as king by God, yet he slowly forgot who his ultimate King was, and began to rely on his own notoriety with the people. Trace this downward spiral in Saul's life using the verses that follow.

10:1-13

13:1-12

15:1-9

28:1-7

3. Samuel makes a brief, passing statement in 1 Samuel 15:17 that actually contains a vital "clue" to Saul's demise. It's in the first part of the verse. Read it carefully. What is Samuel getting at, and why is what he says so vital?

4. Often we attempt to promote ourselves under a veneer of spirituality. How does Saul try to rationalize his own ambition and sin using this tactic (1 Samuel 15:12-21)?

5. There is clear evidence for the motivation behind the downward spiral in Saul's behavior in 1 Samuel 13:11-12 and 15:30. What drove Saul to disregard God?

6. Contrast the following people's perspective on notoriety with that of Saul's.

• John the Baptist (Luke 1:76,80; 3:15-16; John 3:23, 26-30):

• The apostle Paul (Philippians 1:15-18):

• Jesus Christ (Mark 9:33-40):

LEARNING FROM SAUL

Saul began his career with a sense of awe at what God had done in selecting him to be the first king of Israel. It was an honor, and Saul was humbly grateful at first. But he slowly adopted an exaggerated view of his own importance and skill. And in so doing, he lost sight of a vital principle: No matter what the position, a child of God is always first and foremost a servant of God.

Saul enjoyed the title "King of Israel," but forgot the role of "servant of God" upon which it rested. Soon he was merely going through the motions of spirituality, but they lacked any real meaning because he had divorced himself from their proper source. He coveted the praises of men and spurned the approval of God. He forgot that he was once "small in his own eyes," and instead grew to enjoy being "big" in the eyes of others.

But the story of Saul is not simply one more tragic biblical biography. It is an illustration of a negative tendency within each of us. We tend to gravitate toward appreciation and applause, and may even be willing to eventually exchange the commendation of God for the plaudits of our peers. We, too, want to be noticed, respected, and popular. And even though these aspirations may appear harmless at first glance, if left alone they will blossom into bitter fruit.

APPLICATION QUESTIONS

7. Is it possible for a Christian to gain "notoriety" with God—to impress Him the way we do other people? Explain. *NO! He knows our hearts even better than we do.*

8. Saul was abruptly elevated into a position of notoriety rather than being slowly shaped into the position. What principles about aspiring to leadership and appointing leadership can you glean from the story of his life?

• Principles about aspiring to leadership:
God places people in leadership & can just as easily remove them.

• Principles about appointing leaders:

- choose people mature in the Lord
- " " who remember they are
servants of the Lord.

9. Below, describe two spheres of your own life where you see yourself seeking to be noticed, and analyze briefly how you've gone about it.

Because of low self-esteem, I thought if I learned a lot (i.e. college, learning different instruments, etc) people would notice & admire me.

10. What are some major things that you have said or done in order to make yourself "look good" by attaching a veneer of spiritual significance to your words or actions?

11. Look back at your responses to questions 9 and 10. In light of this study, what changes do you feel you need to make in your life? How do you plan to make them?

The Lord has made me content for now where I am.
Being a mother has boosted my self-esteem a lot + having a wonderful supportive husband.

12. Perhaps you have actually driven certain people to seek to be noticed by consciously or unconsciously withholding commendation and praise from them. If so, what can you do about it?

I'm a quiet person — one not to "rock the boat". So I say very little, but I should praise or commend when I see praiseworthy actions, etc.

SCRIPTURE MEMORY

The trap of notoriety—1 Samuel 15:24
Christ's prescription for notoriety—Mark 9:35

9. THE TEN SPIES

The Corrosive Power of Negativism

ABIDING PRINCIPLE

When you constantly complain, you poison others' joy
and turn their gaze away from God.

*A cynic is a man who knows the price of everything and the
value of nothing.* —Oscar Wilde

LOOKING AT THE TEN SPIES

The story of the Jews' exodus from Egyptian oppres-
sion and bondage is saturated with the mystical and
the miraculous. From the death of all of the Egyptians'
firstborn to the defeat of an entire army at the shores of
the Red Sea, God faithfully and dramatically demon-
strated His power. Perhaps that is why we frequently
find ourselves becoming impatient with the implacable
and stiff-necked multitude when we read of their further rebellions in Scripture.

Though their "family scrapbook of failure" is
peppered with portraits of ungodly behavior, the best
example is certainly their response to God at the very
border of the Promised Land. At Kadesh Barnea the

63

nation of Israel passed the point of no return in their sin and rebellion. In fact, what happened there was ultimately responsible for the death of an entire generation and the forty-year postponement of their entrance into the land of milk and honey.

Although most people are familiar with the outcome — death and delay — few are aware of exactly how such a tragedy came to pass. Understanding the causes of this massive failure and sin is essential, for in the final analysis we may find ourselves more similar to the people of Israel than different!

SCRIPTURE Numbers 13:1–14:38

STUDY QUESTIONS

1. Though the spies entered Canaan as a single group, after forty days they returned as two distinct groups with conflicting stories from their journey. From Numbers 13:26-33, describe:

   • Joshua and Caleb's conclusions.

   Positive

   • The other ten spies' conclusions.

   negative

2. Look at Numbers 13:30 and 14:6-9. What did Joshua and Caleb possess that the others lacked, which was responsible for their different conclusions?

   Faith that God would be with them to give them the land

3. Trace the impact that ten men had on a nation of nearly three million. Reconstruct this digression of behavior, using the Scriptures that follow.

Verses	Behavior
13:1-2	Leaders to be chosen to explore the land.
13:21-27	Explored land + gathered cluster of grapes where 2 men needed to carry it. Reported land "flow[s] with milk + honey".
13:28-29	Reported how powerful the people were + how well fortified towns are.
13:31	Declare no way to attack because people are stronger
13:32	Spread bad report about the land
14:1	weeping caused by the reports
14:2-3	Grumbling among people against Moses + Aaron
14:4,10	People want new leader + want to stone Moses + Aaron
14:26-31	God's judgment falls upon the people for complaining.

4. Ten men were able to influence a nation by their negativism. What do you think may also be a natural tendency of people (the nation) that explains why the negativism spread so effectively and quickly?

Prone to grumbling & complaining

5. The impact of a person's attitudes and comments on those around him is something God is very concerned about. Examine the Scripture passages below and write out one central truth from each that relates to negativism.

Deuteronomy 20:1,8 *Fear causes a disheartening in others.*

Proverbs 18:21 *Those who are negative thrive on words that pull one downward.*

Matthew 12:36
Careless words must be accounted for.

Hebrews 12:15
Bitter roots cause trouble & defile

James 3:2 *Faulty words keep us from keeping our bodies in check & from perfection.*

James 3:5
Negative words may seem small, but cause a lot of damage

6. God makes an interesting statement about Caleb in Numbers 14:24. What is it, and how is it related to Paul's command to all Christians in Philippians 2:14-15? *Caleb had a different spirit + followed God wholeheartedly. He didn't complain + was considered what Paul said we would be w/o complaining: "blameless + pure. children of God w/o fault..."*

LEARNING FROM THE TEN SPIES

A dozen men heard the same instructions, made the same journey, and saw the same sights. Yet they returned deeply divided over what it all meant. Ten were convinced that they would soon be dead, along with their friends and families. Two saw difficulty overshadowed by God's promised blessing. Joshua and Caleb had "a different spirit" from the other ten spies, who seemed content to falter and constrained to complain.

The negativism of the ten not only eclipsed the message of hope proclaimed by the two, it spread quickly like spilled oil over the outlook of an entire nation! Soon the very people who had witnessed one miracle after another since they had left Egypt were actually extolling the benefits of their former bondage!

What happened at Kadesh Barnea is tragic. But an equally serious issue there is that the murmuring and complaining of ten men eventually poisoned the hopes of millions. And that poison didn't perish in the Palestinian desert. It's still with us today!

APPLICATION QUESTIONS

7. Before the ten spies began their grumbling, they had to first let go of their understanding of God's character. Following are a number of possible areas where you might habitually grumble or complain. Check all that apply, and in the space provided alongside, write out what you've had to neglect about God's character in order to embrace your complaint.

Area	What You've Forgotten About God
❑ Your health.	
☑ Your vocation.	He is omnipotent + omnicent
☑ Your income.	He will provide all my needs.
❑ Your looks.	
❑ Your weight.	
❑ Your age.	
❑ Your friend(s).	
❑ Your boss.	
❑ Your spouse.	
❑ Your children.	
☑ Your pastor.	God is the one who buildsmen up + tears them down.
❑ Your church.	

Area	What You've Forgotten About God
❑ Your status.	
❑ Your success.	
❑ Your free time.	
❑ Your past.	
❑ Your present circumstances.	

8. Look back over your answers above. If you've checked more than four, it is possible that you are a negative person. Ask a close friend:

   • if he or she perceives you as a negative person.
   • if so, if he or she would be willing to help you eliminate the negativism.

9. According to Ephesians 4:29 and 1 Thessalonians 5:18, what should characterize your attitude and speech?

   We need to build others up w/ our words. Don't let words that tear down come out of your mouth. We need to give thanks to God no matter what circumstances are in our lives.

10. Like the ten spies, we too have the power to "poi-son" the outlook of others by our negative attitude and comments.

   • Is another person "poisoning" your opinion of something or someone by his or her continual negative comments? Perhaps you need to politely ask that person to stop.

   • Are you "poisoning" others' opinion of someone or something by your continual negativism? You need to stop. Write out below what you need to do and how you plan to go about it.

   Read & Study the Bible more & give all my problems over to Dad to take care of.

11. Perhaps you find it easier to talk about what's bad in your life more than about what's good. Write out ten things about your life right now that are posi-tive. Pick two, and talk about them today to your normal daily associates.

   - Wonderful, careing husband
   - Healthy, happy Child
   - Home
   - job

SCRIPTURE MEMORY

Don't complain—Philippians 2:14-15
Be thankful—1 Thessalonians 5:18

10. JOSEPH

Victim or Victor?

ABIDING PRINCIPLE

For the obedient child of God, tragedy, trauma, and testing are all opportunities for growth from a sovereign and loving heavenly Father.

Adversity is God's university. — Paul Evans

LOOKING AT JOSEPH

Jacob's twelve sons became the nation of Israel. Each of their lives is a drama unto itself. But his second-youngest son's life contains lessons of lasting importance. The story of Joseph is vibrant, punctuated with sibling rivalry, romance, sexual and political intrigue, friendship, and cunning.

Joseph was frequently mistreated, misunderstood, and misjudged. Joseph experienced the extremes of life. He was acquainted with the ecstasy of success, the agony of deceit, and the devastation of disgrace. In the words of the apostle Paul, Joseph indeed knew how to handle having very little and how to handle having plenty (Philippians 4:12). And all of the many painful circumstances in this young man's life can be traced directly to the deeds and decisions of others!

If Joseph lived today, we would probably consider him a "victim" of unjust circumstances—a man whose personal "rights" had been ignored or violated. But how did Joseph see himself? And more importantly, was he really a "victim"?

SCRIPTURE Genesis 37:1-28, 39:1-23, 40:1-23

STUDY QUESTIONS

---

1. Below are the accounts of three of the most traumatic events in the life of Joseph. Examine each one thoughtfully and write out:

   • a brief description of the circumstances.
   • who you think was responsible, and why.
   • Joseph's probable thoughts and feelings.

EVENT 1—Genesis 37:18-28 (see also 37:3-4)

The circumstances: *Jacob loved Joseph more than any of his other sons ~ because of this his brothers hated him. They decided instead of killing him to sell him to the Ishmaelites headed for Egypt.*

The "culprit(s)": *Joseph's brothers.*

Joseph's thoughts and feelings:
angry, fearful

72

EVENT 2—Genesis 39:1-23

The circumstances: Joseph was put in charge of Potiphar's house. His wife wanted Joseph, but he ran from her leaving his cloak. She told a lie that landed Joseph in jail.

The "culprit(s)":

Potiphar's wife

Joseph's thoughts and feelings:

Calm, trusting God

EVENT 3—Genesis 40:1-23

The circumstances: Joseph finds favor in prison + is put in charge of Pharoah's cupbearer + baker, who had offended Pharoah. Each has a dream that Joseph interprets correctly. He asks the cupbearer to remember him when he got out of prison, but he forgot all about Joseph.

The "culprit(s)": The cupbearer

Joseph's thoughts and feelings:

wrongly put in prison, wants to be freed.

73

2. If you had been Joseph's best friend, quietly observing what happened to him at Dothan, Potiphar's house, and the Pharaoh's prison, would you have considered Joseph a "victim" — someone whose "rights" had been violated? Explain.

Yes, because I probably wouldn't be able to see the whole picture God was laying out.

3. How did Joseph view the tragic circumstances of his life and the violation of his "rights" (Genesis 45:1-5, 50:18-20)? *He believed that God used all his tragic circumstances to bring about good — he was able to save many from dying of starvation during the famine*

4. If a contemporary person were somehow transported back in time to observe the scene at the Cross of Golgotha without remembering anything about the biblical account, would he consider Jesus of Nazareth a "victim" and the crucifixion a tragic human error? Explain. (Be honest!)

Probably, unless he understood what God's plan was all about.

5. What did Peter, filled with the Holy Spirit, consider to be the main reason for the crucifixion (Acts 4:27-28)?

God's power + will was decided before to do.

6. If Joseph and Jesus were both living a life of true obedience to God, in what sense could they not be "victims"?

They were used of God for the purpose of saving lives, + they in turn were blessed.

LEARNING FROM JOSEPH

Joseph's response to the injustice, cruelty and "bad luck" he faced and endured is an encouraging yet sobering reminder that God is sovereign in the lives of His children. Joseph's statement to his brothers, "You intended to harm me, but God intended it for good" (Genesis 50:20), is a powerful truth about life within the circumference of God's family.

How do you think Joseph would be counseled today? Would you and I assist him to arrive at the same conclusions he reached on his own? Or would we encourage him to "stand on his rights," and blame his father and brothers, or Potiphar's wife, or the Pharaoh's cupbearer?

Victimization—the ideology that I am a "victim" of others—is a twentieth-century catchall for explaining life's pain. Yet, while providing a temporary balm for our emotional aches, it subtly destroys our confidence in God's competence and the conviction that He really cares.

7. Joseph's statement, "God intended it for good," was perhaps somewhat easier to make because he actually got to see and be part of the "good." But what about circumstances in which no good seems to come? Are the principles from Joseph's life still valid? Explain.

8. Can you think of any examples of characters in the Bible where no "good" came to them (in this life)?

9. As Christians, when we blame other people or difficult cimcumstances for our pain, are we really making an unconscious attempt to blame God? Explain. (See Job 2:9-10.)

10. Describe a recent circumstance in your life where you concluded (or were told) that you had been a "victim" or that your rights had been violated.

11. Perhaps you know someone who feels victimized. How can you creatively and sensitively share with this person the principles from this lesson?

12. Spend some time in prayer, telling the Lord about an incorrect perspective you've had about something in your past, especially if you've felt victimized or unjustly treated by Him. Ask Him to help you see it in the context of His sovereign love.

SCRIPTURE MEMORY
_____

God's purposes in pain—James 1:2-4
Our responsibility in pain—1 Peter 4:19

11. JESUS

Facing the Death of Someone You Love

ABIDING PRINCIPLE

For the Christian, there is a valid place for both hope
and grief when facing the death of a loved one.

*We understand death for the first time when he puts his hand
upon one whom we love.* — Anne L. de Stael

LOOKING AT JESUS

Death is the final frontier of certainty for man. We
have to reckon with its reality at some point in our
lives. Sometimes we challenge its power without fear
of reprisal and other times we tremble as its shadow
approaches. Perhaps it is the uncertainty of what comes
after death that is so unnerving. For most, it is a dark
corridor into the unknown, a thief of all that is dear in
this life.

But what about the child of God? Shouldn't our per-
ception of death be distinctly different? The resurrection
of Jesus Christ in history provides us with the assurance
that this life is not the end, but merely a doorway into
eternity. So Christians need not fear death.

But how are we to face the death of someone we love—a spouse, child, or dear friend? What is the biblical response to such a tragedy? Fortunately for us, we can observe Jesus as He faced the death of someone He loved. His response is as relevant today as it was in the dusty Palestinian countryside nearly 2000 years ago.

SCRIPTURE John 11:1-44

STUDY QUESTIONS

1. What evidence is there in this story that Jesus actually planned on Lazarus dying (see especially 11:3-7,11-14)? *"for God's glory ..." Jn 11:4*

In what Jesus says, and does. I.E. waiting a couple more days before going to Lazarus. He knows he is going to raise him from the dead.

2. a. What is the assumption behind the comments of Martha, Mary, and the Jews from Jerusalem (John 11:21,32,37)?

They knew Jesus could have healed Lazarus if he were still alive, but they hadn't considered Jesus could raise the dead.

   b. Do you think we ever make similar kinds of assumptions when a loved one dies?

   c. What is comforting about Jesus' response to their accusations (see verses 23,25-26,33,35, and 38)? (Note what He didn't do, as well as what He did do.)

He was moved and told them he was going to raise Lazarus, even though they didn't believe or think he could.

80

3. Would you describe Jesus' response to the situation from the time He met the women until He arrived at the tomb as "grief"? Explain. *No, he knew Lazarus would rise. He was disappointed & saddened in the people's unbelief.*

4. Paul often stresses the fact that we can place our hope and confidence in the resurrection of our bodies (see Romans 8:11). But according to 1 Thessalonians 4:13-14, does Paul discourage Christians from grieving over the death of others? Should we make a distinction between the death of believers and the death of nonbelievers? Explain. *Yes, Paul says we will see believers again. Nonbelievers unfortunately have a sadder ending & will be tormented eternally, and in that case we cannot rejoice when a nonbeliever dies.*

5. When Jesus met Martha and she blamed Him for her brother's death, Jesus responded with a statement of hope (John 11:23). But Martha saw it merely as a rote statement of doctrine (11:24). Jesus' next words to Martha (11:25-26) are very significant. What was He trying to get her to see? *That life comes from Himself; eternal and physical life.*

LEARNING FROM JESUS

Jesus allowed Lazarus to die so that He could teach a lesson on eternal life. But the interim period between Lazarus' death and resurrection also contains valuable insights for us today.

We learn from Jesus' dealings with Martha and Mary that God is touched by our emotions in the face of the loss of someone we dearly love. We see in our Lord's response to the trauma and pain of the sisters and their friends genuine empathy and grief over the ravaging effects of sin and death. Jesus wept real tears. He didn't eulogize, or minimize their pain. Instead, He wept with them! If the Son of God showed such deep grief, can we do less?

But, Jesus also spoke words of hope in the midst of their pain. Not the idle recitation of Bible verses and theological doctrines, but a living hope rooted in the Author of Life Himself.

God wants to reassure us that we can grieve with a sense of hope when another believer dies. Consequently, as we face the inevitable and unpredictable death of those we love, we can do so with the assurance that our pain is "okay" with God, and also that death is not the "end." Our loved one is absent, not gone. As Christians, we can feel pain and sorrow over death, but we must also maintain an eternal perspective (2 Corinthians 4:16-18, Colossians 3:1-4). We can rejoice in the fact that our reunion with our brothers and sisters in Christ is as certain as their departure.

Knowing all of this is comforting. But how can we use it?

APPLICATION QUESTIONS

6. Based on what you've discovered from this study, defend this statement: "For the Christian, grief and hope are both legitimate responses to the death of a fellow believer."

7. How can this principle help you cope with:

   • a recent death?

   • a possible future death?

   • a friend who has lost a loved one?

8. What do you think are the dangers of getting "stuck" on either side of this delicate balance?

   • Getting stuck on the hope side:

   • Getting stuck on the grief side:

9. Does this principle apply to facing the death of nonbelievers, too? Explain.

10. Based on what you've discovered from this lesson, make a list of things you think should not be said or done to someone who is facing the death of a loved one.

SCRIPTURE MEMORY
_____

Death is not the end—John 11:25-26
Grieving with hope—1 Thessalonians 4:13-14

12. THE HOLY SPIRIT

A Misunderstood "Counselor"?

ABIDING PRINCIPLE

In your rush to find your way out of difficulty, you may be overlooking the larger purposes of God.

Every time we say "I believe in the Holy Spirit," we mean that we believe there is a living God able and willing to enter human personality and change it. —J. B. Phillips

LOOKING AT THE HOLY SPIRIT

Many people have questions about who the Holy Spirit is. He is given a number of titles in the Bible, including "Counselor" (NIV), "Comforter" (KJV), and "Helper" (NASB). These three titles are ways of expressing the Greek word *parakletos*. A very similar Greek word is translated "encourage" elsewhere in Scripture (Philippians 2:1).

Unfortunately we sometimes end up with the wrong impression of the Holy Spirit because of our modern ways of thinking of these terms. Nowadays when we use words like "encourage" and "comfort," we tend to have images of solace, sympathy, and compassion. Consequently, the

Holy Spirit—"the Comforter"—is pictured as One who is deeply moved by our pain and relates to us mostly on the level of our feelings.

"Encouragement" is a modern buzzword for emotional consolation. While this is of course true, it is not the primary meaning of the words in the *parakletos* word family, nor is it the focus of the Spirit's work in our lives. In some cases, it may be the opposite! The English word "comfort" used to mean to *fortify* or *strengthen*. The word "encourage" used to mean to *infuse with courage*.

In short, the word *parakletos* involves providing strength more than solace, courage more than consolation, and stamina more than sympathy. It characterizes a kind of help that enables those on the verge of collapse to stand and remain standing.

Seeing this distinction and understanding its implications is essential because not only will it affect whether or not we will look to God the Holy Spirit as our first option in times of discouragement and depression, but also what manner of help we will expect from Him when we do.

SCRIPTURE John 14:15-27, 16:5-15; Romans 8

STUDY QUESTIONS

1. a. What do the following verses collectively say about our tendency when facing difficult and painful circumstances (Isaiah 65:2, Jeremiah 2:13, Galatians 3:3)? *Pursuing own imaginations, forsaken the Lord, Attain goal by human effort, dug own cisterns*

    Our tendency is to forget about the Lord, and try to do things in our own strength.

    b. Why do you think we tend to do this?

    Human nature declares "Seeing is believing". Since we are initially spiritually blind we want to see for ourselves that things are done.

86

2. a. God's description of one who tries to "fix" things by his own strength is found in Jeremiah 17:5-6. Rewrite this passage in your own words.

This person will be cursed with spiritual blindness not being able to see help when it comes to him & unable to see that he is living in spiritual bankruptcy.

b. Why do you think things turn out this way?

3. As we saw earlier, the "comfort" of the Holy Spirit consists more of fortitude and courage than of solace and sympathy. Write out what the following verses have to say about the different areas in which the Spirit "fortifies" us, and how or why He goes about it.

Verses	Comfort From the Spirit
Psalm 73:21-26	*Guides with His counsel*
Romans 15:4	*gives hope through endurance & the encouragement of the Scriptures.*
Romans 8:26-27	*intercedes for us in our weakness.*
Colossians 4:8	*encourages by another fellow believer (specifically sent)*
Hebrews 3:12-13	*encourages daily so hearts will not be hardened.*

87

4. In 2 Corinthians 1:3-4, God provides us with a
powerful statement about why He wants to comfort
us. What is it, and what principle can you draw
from this passage about Christians and pain?

*God wants to comfort us so that we will
know how to comfort others who need it.
We as Christians have a purpose in our
pain: To allow God to touch + comfort us
in order to give of ourselves to another
hurting Christian*

LEARNING FROM THE HOLY SPIRIT

It is certainly true that God is our compassionate and
loving Father and that He wills what is best for His
children. *But* it is also true that often His desire is to
strengthen us through the Holy Spirit in the midst of
our difficulty and pain rather than merely to deliver us
from it. Sometimes our circumstances are the very vehi-
cles of growth and change. He promises us His strength
and provides it for us through His Word, His people,
and His Holy Spirit.

One of God's reasons for comforting us in our
distress is so that we can comfort others in similar
circumstances. For the Christian, pain sometimes has
a measurably good purpose. Our greatest temptation
when we face painful circumstances is to prefer consolation over true comfort, and thereby we often miss the
real ministry of the Holy Spirit.

APPLICATION QUESTIONS

5. List, in order of your own preference (1 = first), the
sources you tend to look to or run to for comfort or
guidance when in need. Several examples are given.
(You may also want to ask someone close to use
this same list to give an outside perspective on your
inclinations.)

#1 _God_____

#2 _spouse_____

#3 _son - comfort_

#4 _Scriptures___

#5 _friend_____

#6 _____

#7 _____

#8 _____

#9 _____

- a close friend
- a spouse
- God (in prayer)
- a counselor or therapist
- your child(ren)
- the Scriptures
- your pastor
- your parent(s)

6. Now, using what you've learned from this lesson, prioritize your list one more time, this time as you believe it *should* be.

#1 _God_____

#2 _Scriptures___

#3 _Husband_____

#4 _Pastor_____

#5 _Parents_____

#6 _Close friend_

#7 _____

#8 _____

#9 _____

89

7. What do you normally expect the Holy Spirit to do for you when you go to God during difficulty?

Give me peace and assurance that God is in control

8. Describe how you have been able to minister genuine *comfort* and *encouragement* to someone else because of a painful experience in your own life.

9. Look back over your answers to questions 5 and 6. Is there any indication of a need for a change in your behavior during difficulty? If so, what change? How do you plan to go about it?

SCRIPTURE MEMORY

Our need for encouragement—2 Peter 1:3
Our source of encouragement—Romans 15:13

SMALL-GROUP MATERIALS FROM NAVPRESS

BIBLE STUDY SERIES

DESIGN FOR DISCIPLESHIP
GOD IN YOU
GOD'S DESIGN FOR THE FAMILY
INSTITUTE OF BIBLICAL
  COUNSELING SERIES

LEARNING TO LOVE SERIES
LIFECHANGE
LOVE ONE ANOTHER
STUDIES IN CHRISTIAN LIVING
THINKING THROUGH DISCIPLESHIP

TOPICAL BIBLE STUDIES

Becoming a Woman of
  Excellence
Becoming a Woman of Freedom
Becoming a Woman of Purpose
The Blessing Study Guide
Celebrating Life
Growing in Christ
Growing Strong in God's Family
Homemaking
Intimacy with God

Loving Your Husband
Loving Your Wife
A Mother's Legacy
Strategies for a Successful
  Marriage
Surviving Life in the Fast Lane
To Run and Not Grow Tired
To Walk and Not Grow Weary
What God Does When Men Pray
When the Squeeze Is On

BIBLE STUDIES WITH COMPANION BOOKS

Bold Love
The Feminine Journey
From Bondage to Bonding
Hiding from Love
Inside Out
The Masculine Journey
The Practice of Godliness
The Pursuit of Holiness

Secret Longings of the
  Heart
Spiritual Disciplines
Tame Your Fears
Transforming Grace
Trusting God
What Makes a Man?
The Wounded Heart
Your Work Matters to God

RESOURCES

Brothers!
How to Lead Small Groups
Jesus Cares for Women
The Small Group Leaders
  Training Course

Topical Memory System (KJV/NIV
  and NASB/NKJV)
Topical Memory System: Life
  Issues (KJV/NIV and
  NASB/NKJV)

VIDEO PACKAGES

Bold Love
Hope Has Its Reasons
Inside Out
Living Proof

Parenting Adolescents
Unlocking Your Sixth Suitcase
Your Home, A Lighthouse